Voices

D1226058

Voices

poems by

Lucille Clifton

■

american poets continuum series, no. 112

BOA Editions, Ltd. ■ Rochester, NY ■ 2008

10 11 12 4 3 2

For information about permission to reuse any material from this book please
contact The Permissions Company at www.permissionscompany.com or e-mail
permdude@eclipse.net.

Publications by BOA Editions, Ltd.—a not-for-profit corporation under section 501
(c) (3) of the United States Internal Revenue Code—are made possible with funds
from a variety of sources, including public funds from the New York State Council
on the Arts, a state agency; the Literature Program of the National Endowment for
the Arts; the County of Monroe, NY; the Lannan Foundation for support of the
Lannan Translations Selection Series; the Sonia Raiziss Giop Charitable Foundation;
the Mary S. Mulligan Charitable Trust; the Rochester Area Community Foundation;
the Arts & Cultural Council for Greater Rochester; the Steeple-Jack Fund; the Ames-
Amzalak Memorial Trust in memory of Henry Ames, Semon Amzalak and Dan
Amzalak; the TCA Foundation; and contributions from many individuals nationwide.

See Colophon on page 64 for special individual acknowledgments.

Cover Design: Geri McCormick
Cover Art: "Mystical World" by Steve Carpenter
Interior Design and Composition: Richard Foerster
Manufacturing: Thomson-Shore
BOA Logo: Mirko

Library of Congress Cataloging-in-Publication Data

Clifton, Lucille, 1936–
Voices : poems / by Lucille Clifton. — 1st ed.
    p. cm. — (American poets continuum series ; no. 112)
ISBN 978–1–934414–11–8 (alk. hardcover) — ISBN 978–1–934414–12–5
(pbk. : alk. paper)
I. Title.
PS3553.L45V55 2008
811'.54—dc22
                                    2008037162

BOA Editions, Ltd.
Thom Ward, Editor/Production
Peter Conners, Editor/Marketing
Melissa Hall, Development Director/Office Manager
Bernadette Catalana, BOA Board Chair
A. Poulin, Jr., Founder (1938 – 1996)
250 North Goodman Street, Suite 306
Rochester, NY 14607
www.boaeditions.org

NATIONAL
ENDOWMENT
FOR THE ARTS

State of the Arts

NYSCA

Contents

■ **hearing**

■ **being heard**

■ ten oxherding pictures

for my little bird
and
my beamish boy

"all goodbye ain't gone"

hearing

"marley was dead to begin with"

from *A Christmas Carol*

then in trenchtown and in babylon
the sound of marleys ghost
rose and began to fill the air
like in the christmas tale

his spirit shuddered and was alive
again   his dreadful locks
thick in the voices of his children

ziggy and i and i marley again
standing and swaying
everything gonna be alright
little darling
no woman   no cry

■

aunt jemima

white folks say i remind them
of home   i who have been homeless
all my life except for their
kitchen cabinets

i who have made the best
of everything
pancakes   batter for chicken
my life

the shelf on which i sit
between the flour and cornmeal
is thick with dreams
oh how i long for

my own syrup
rich as blood
my true nephews   my nieces
my kitchen   my family
my home

■

uncle ben

mother guineas favorite son
knew rice and that was almost
all he knew
not where he was
not why
not who were the pale sons
of a pale moon
who had brought him here
rice   rice   rice
and so he worked the river
worked as if born to it
thinking only now and then
of himself   of the sun
of afrika

■

cream of wheat

sometimes at night
we stroll the market aisles
ben and jemima and me   they
walk in front   remembering this and that
i lag behind
trying to remove my chefs cap
wondering about what ever pictured me
then left me personless
Rastus
i read in an old paper
i was called rastus
but no mother ever
gave that to her son   toward dawn
we return to our shelves
our boxes   ben and jemima and me
we pose and smile   i simmer   what
is my name

■

horse prayer

why was i born to balance
this two-leg
on my back   to carry
across my snout
his stocking of oat and apple
why   i pray to You
Father Of What Runs And Swims
in the name of the fenceless
field   when he declares himself
master
does he not understand my
neigh

■

raccoon prayer

oh Master Of All Who Take And Wash
And Eat   lift me away at the end into evening
forever   into sanctified crumples of paper
and peelings curled over my hand
i have scavenged as i must
among the hairless
now welcome this bandit into the kingdom
just as you made him
barefoot and faithful and clean

■

dog's god

has lifted dog
on four magnificent legs
has blessed him with fur
against the cold
and blessed him with
two-legs to feed him
and clean his waste
gods dog
spins and tumbles
in the passion
of his praise

■

albino

for kathy

we sat
in the stalled
car
watching him
watch us
his great pink
antlers
branched
his pink eyes
fixed
on the joy
of the black woman
and the white one
laughing together
and he smiled
at the sometime
wonderfulness
of other

■

mataoka

(actual name of pocahontas)

in the dream was white men
walking up from the river

in the dream was our land
stolen away and our horses
and our names

in the dream was my father
fighting to save us   in the dream
the pipe was broken

and i was leaning my body
across the whimpering
white man

if our father loves revenge
more than he loves his children
spoke the dream

we need to know it now

■

witko

aka crazy horse

the man
who wore a blue stone
behind his ear
did not dance
dreamed
clear fields
and redmen everywhere
woke and braided
his curling brown hair
as his enchanted horse
who woke with him
prepared
whispering
Hoka Hay brother
it is a good day
to die

■

what haunts him

that moment after the bartender
refused to serve the dark marine
and the three white skinned others
just sat there   that moment
before they rose and followed
their nappy brother
out into the USA they were
willing to die to defend
then

■

my grandfather's lullaby

pretty little nappy baby
rockin in that chair
theys a world outside
the window
and somebody in it hates you

let me hold you baby
and love you all i can
better to hear it from papa
than learn it all alone

■

"you have been my tried and trusted friend"

said the coal miners son
to the chippers daughter
then turned his head and died
and she and their children rose
and walked behind the coffin
to the freeway
                    after a while
she started looking at
other womens husbands other
womens sons but she had been
tried and trusted once and
though once is never enough
she knew two may be too
many

■

lu
1942

what i know is
this is called gravel
you must not eat it
you must not throw it
at your brother

what i know is
over there is our house
our sidewalk too
there is no grass   grass
is for the white folks section

what i know is
something is coming   mama
calls it war   calls it change
mama loves me   daddy
loves me too much

what i know is
this is in the middle
i am in the middle
come in   come in my mama calls
you can't stay there forever

■

sorrows

who would believe them winged
who would believe they could be

beautiful   who would believe
they could fall so in love with mortals

that they would attach themselves
as scars attach and ride the skin

sometimes we hear them in our dreams
rattling their skulls   clicking

their bony fingers
they have heard me beseeching

as i whispered into my own
cupped hands   enough   not me again

but who can distinguish
one human voice

amid such choruses
of desire

■

being heard

this is what i know
my mother went mad
in my fathers house
for want of tenderness

this is what i know
some womens days
are spooned out
in the kitchen of their lives

this is why i know
the gods
are men

■

my father hasn't come back
to apologize   i have stood
and waited almost sixty years
so different from the nights
i wedged myself between
the mattress and the wall

i do not hate him
i assure myself
only his probing fingers
i have to teach you
he one time whispered
more to himself than me

i am seventy-two-years-old
dead man and in another city
standing with my daughters   granddaughters
trying to understand you
trying to help them understand
the sticks and stones of love

■

dad

consider the raw potato
wrapped in his dress sock
consider his pocket
heavy with loose change
consider his printed list
of whitemens names

for beating her
and leaving no bruises
for bus fare
for going bail
for vouching for him
he would say

consider
he would say
the gods might
understand
a man like me

■

faith

my father was so sure
that afternoon
he put on his Sunday suit
and waited at the front porch
one hand in his pocket
the other gripping his hat
to greet the end of the world

waited there patient as the eclipse
ordained the darkening
of everything
the house   the neighborhood we knew
the world   his hopeful eyes the only
glowing things on purdy street

■

afterblues

"i hate to see the evening sun go down"

my mothers son
died in his sleep

and so did mine
both of them found

though years apart
hands folded in

unexpected prayer
cold on a bed

of trouble   my brother
my son

my mama was right
theys blues
in the night

■

the dead do dream

scattered   they dream of gathering
each perfect ash to each
so that where there was blindness
there is sight
and all the awkward bits
discarded

if they have been folded
into boxes
they dream themselves spilling
out and away
their nails grown long and
menacing

some of them dream they are asleep
on ordinary pillows
they rise to look around
their ordinary rooms
to walk among the lives
of their heedless kin

■

"in 1844 explorers John Fremont and Kit Carson discovered Lake Tahoe"

—Lodge guidebook

in 1841 Washoe children
swam like otters in the lake
their mothers rinsed red beans
in 1842 Washoe warriors began to dream
dried bones and hollow reeds
they woke clutching their shields
in 1843 Washoe elders began to speak
of grass hunched in fear and
thunder sticks over the mountain
in 1844 Fremont and Carson

■

mirror

one day
we will look into the mirror
and the great nation standing there
will shake its head and frown
they way babies do who
are just born
and cant remember
why they asked for just
these people   just this chance
and when we close our eyes
against regret
we will be left alone
in the wrong image   not understanding
what we are or what we
had hoped to be

■

6/27/06

pittsburgh   you in white
like the ghost
of all my desires   my heart
stopped and renamed itself
i was thirty-six
today i am seventy   my eyes
have dimmed from looking for you
my body has swollen from swallowing
so much love

■

in amira's room

you are not nearly light enough
i whisper to myself
staring up at the stars
on amiras ceiling

you are my lightest grandchild
she would smile
crazy lady who loved me more
of course

shining among my cousins
in my maryjanes
sure that i could one day
lift from the darkness

from the family holding me
to what the world would call
unbearable
i lie here now

under my godchilds ceiling
grandma gone   cousins all gone
the dark world still
smug still visible
among the stars

■

for maude

what i am forgetting doubles everyday
what i am remembering
is you   is us aging
though you called me girl
i can feel us   white haired
nappy and not
listening to marvin
both of us wondering
whats going on   all of us
wondering   oh darlin girl
what   what   what

■

highway 89 toward tahoe

a congregation
of red rocks
sits at attention
watching the water
the trees among them
rustle hosanna
hosanna
something stalls the rental car
something moves us
something in the river
Christ
rowing for our lives

■

ten oxherding pictures

a meditation on ten oxherding pictures

here are the hands
they are still
if i ask them to rise
they will rise
if i ask them to turn
they will turn in an arc
of perfect understanding
they have allowed me only such
privilege as owed to flesh
or bone   no more   they know
they belong to the ox

■   ⁃

1st picture
searching for the ox

they have waited my lifetime for this
something has entered the hands
they stir
the fingers come together
caressing each others tips
in a need beyond desire
until the silence has released
something like a name
they move away   i follow
it is the summons from the ox

■

2nd picture
seeing the traces

as tracks
in the buffalo snow
leading to only
a mirror
and what do they make of that
the hands

or baltimore
voices whispering
in a room where no one sits
except myself

and what do the hands make of that

■

3rd picture
seeing the ox

not the flesh
not the image
of the flesh
not the bone
nor the clicking
of the bone
not the brain
wearing its mask
not the mind
nor its disguises
not this me
not that me
now here where
no thing is defined
we are coming to the ox

■

4th picture
catching the ox

i whisper come
and something comes
i am cautioned by the hands

■

5th picture
herding the ox

the hands refuse to gather
they sit in their pockets as i
command ox and enhance my name
i am lucille who masters ox
ox is the one lucille masters
hands caution me again
what can be herded
is not ox

■

6th picture
coming home on the ox's back

i mount the ox
and we shamble
on toward the city together
our name is inflated
as we move   lucille
who has captured ox
ox who supports lucille
we meet a man who wears
authority   he defines ox
describes him
the man claims ox
i claim the man

■

7th picture
the ox forgotten   leaving the man
alone

· i have been arriving
fifty years   parents
children lovers
have walked with me
eating me like cake
and i am a good baker
somewhere i was going
fifty years
hands shiver in their pockets
dearly beloved
where is ox

■

8th picture
the ox and the man both gone out of sight

man is not ox
i am not ox
no thing is ox
all things are ox

■

9th picture
returning to the origin
back to the source

what comes
when you whisper ox
is not
the ox
ox
begins in silence
and ends
in the folding
of hands

■

10th picture
entering the city
with bliss-bestowing hands

we have come to the gates
of the city
the hands begin to move
i ask of them
only forgiveness
they tremble as they rise

■

end of meditation

what is ox
ox is
what

■

note

Ten Oxherding Pictures is an allegorical series composed as a train-
ing guide for Chinese Buddhist monks. The pictures are attributed to
kaku-an shi-en, twelfth-century Chinese Zen master. I was unaware
of them until after these poems were written. I had only read the
titles of the pictures.

■

acknowledgments

Grateful acknowledgment is made to the editors of of the following journals in which these poems appeared:

Chautauqua Literary Journal: "afterblues," "aunt jemima," "cream of wheat," "faith," "in amira's room," "uncle ben";

Poetry: "sorrows."

■

about the author

Lucille Clifton was born near Buffalo, New York. She is the mother of six children, two of whom are deceased. She is also a grandmother and an aunt. Like her mother, she was born with twelve fingers.

Clifton was the 2007 recipient of the Ruth Lilly Poetry Prize for lifetime achievement from the Poetry Foundation. She is the author of twelve books of poetry, one prose collection, and nineteen books for children. Her collection *Blessing the Boats: New and Selected Poems 1988–2000* received the National Book Award for Poetry. Other honors include an Emmy Award from the American Academy of Television Arts and Sciences, two fellowships from the National Endowment for the Arts, the Shelley Memorial Prize, the Charity Randall Citation, and a Lannan Literary Award. In 1996, she was a National Book Award Finalist for *The Terrible Stories* and was the only poet ever to have two books (*next: new poems* and *good woman: poems and a memoir 1969–1980*) chosen as finalists for the Pulitzer Prize in the same year. Appointed a Chancellor of The Academy of American Poets in 1999 and elected a Fellow in Literature of The American Academy of Arts and Sciences, Clifton currently resides in Columbia, Maryland, and she is a Distinguished Adjunct Professor of Humanities and Friend of St. Marys College. She also holds the Hilda C. Landers Chair in the Liberal Arts at the college.

■

BOA EDITIONS, LTD.
american poets continuum series

Colophon

Voices, poems by Lucille Clifton, is set in a digital version of Optima, the typeface designed by Hermann Zapf in the 1950s for the D. Stempel AG foundry in Frankfurt, Germany. Classically roman in proportion and character, but without serifs, it was based on sixteenth-century graveplates that Zapf had seen on the floor of the Church of Santa Croce in Florence.

The publication of this book is made possible, in part, by the special support of the following individuals:

Anonymous (2) ▪ Kazim Ali ▪ Michael Blumenthal
▪ Susan Burke & Bill Leonardi ▪ Alan & Nancy
Cameros ▪ Gwen & Gary Conners ▪
Dale Davis & Michael Starenko
▪ Susan DeWitt Davie ▪ Peter & Sue Durant ▪
Pete & Bev French ▪ Marla Friedrich
▪ Robert L. Giron ▪ Judy & Dane Gordon ▪
Kip & Debby Hale ▪ Sandi Henschel
▪ Peter & Robin Hursh ▪ Willy & Bob Hursh ▪
X. J. & Dorothy Kennedy ▪ Archie & Pat Kutz
▪ Jason D. Labbe ▪ Jack & Gail Langerak ▪
Dorianne Laux & Joseph Millar
▪ Katherine Lederer ▪ Rosemary & Lewis Lloyd ▪
Dan Meyers ▪ Boo Poulin
▪ John Roche, in memory of Shirley S. Roche ▪
Steven O. Russell & Phyllis Rifkin-Russell
▪ Chris & Sarah Schoettle ▪ Jane Moress Schuster
▪ Vicki & Richard Schwartz ▪ Bob Shea,
in memory of Liam Rector
▪ George & Bonnie Wallace ▪
The Wallack Family ▪ Thomas R. Ward
▪ Patricia D. Ward-Baker ▪ Michael Waters ▪
Pat & Mike Wilder ▪ Glenn & Helen William
▪ Steve & Erica Yunghans ▪ Geraldine Zetzel,
in honor of Kinereth Gensler